BIOMIMICRY

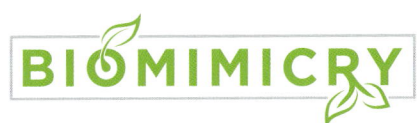

AWESOME INNOVATIONS INSPIRED BY DOLPHINS

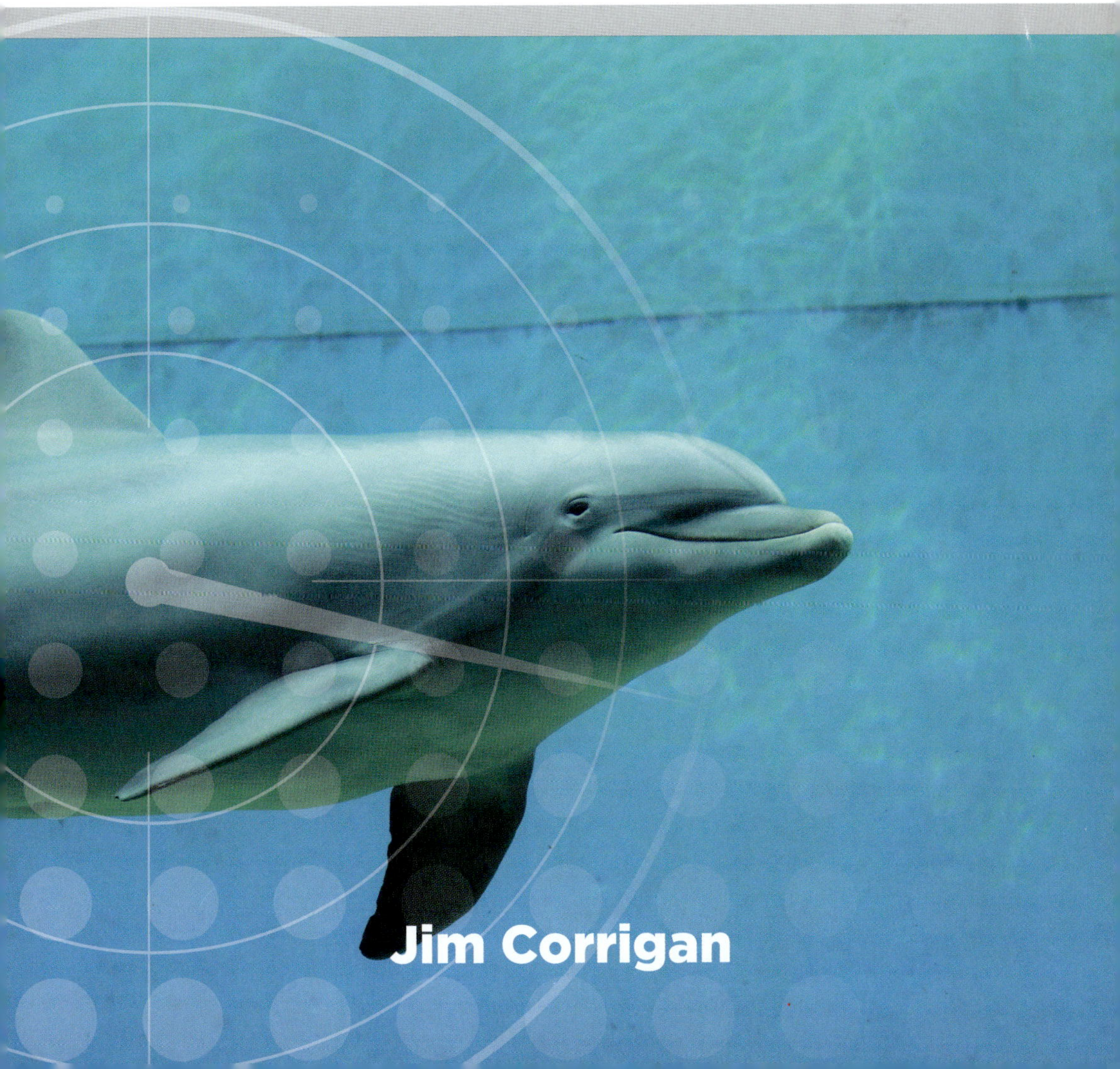

Jim Corrigan

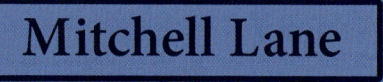

mitchelllane.com

2001 SW 31st Avenue
Hallandale, FL 33009

Copyright © 2021 by Mitchell Lane Publishers. All rights reserved. No part of this book may be reproduced without written permission from the publisher. Printed and bound in the United States of America.

First Edition, 2021.
Author: Jim Corrigan
Designer: Ed Morgan
Editor: Sharon F. Doorasamy

Series: Biomimicry
Title: Awesome Innovations Inspired by Dolphins / by Jim Corrigan

Hallandale, FL : Mitchell Lane Publishers, [2021]

Library bound ISBN: 978-1-68020-605-0
eBook ISBN: 978-1-68020-606-7

PHOTO CREDITS: cover: freepik.com, p. 5 naturelovephotography shutterstock.com, p. 6 JP5\ZOB/WENN/Newscom, p. 7 Yale Cohen on Unsplash, p. 8 Martin Harvey/NHPA/Photoshot/Newscom, p. 9 Nobu Tamura CC-BY-SA-3.0, p. 9 freepik.com, pp. 11-12 freepik.com, p. 13 Album / Florilegius/Newscom, p. 15 shutterstock.com, p. 17 JamesDeMers from Pixabay, p. 19 Public Domain, pp. 22-23 SCIEPRO/SCIENCE PHOTO LIBRARY/Newscom, p. 25 John Milner/ZUMA Press/Newscom, p. 27 Pagie Page on Unsplash

Contents

1. **Swimming Machine** — 4
2. **Ocean of Ideas** — 10
3. **Sea Genius** — 14
4. **Superb Seekers** — 18
5. **Deep Discoveries** — 24

What You Should Know — 28
Want to be an engineer? Architect? Inventor? — 29
Glossary — 30
Online Resources — 31
Further Reading — 31
Index — 32
About the Author — 32

1st CHAPTER

Swimming Machine

The human body does many things well. Swimming is not one of them. Our legs and feet are better suited for land. In water, we move pitifully slow.

A dolphin, on the other hand, is a swimming machine. Dolphins can go more than 20 miles (32 kilometers) per hour. They often keep pace with motorboats.

A dolphin's power comes from its tail, or fluke. Inventor Ted Ciamillo of Athens, Georgia, made a fluke for humans. His rubber dolphin tail attaches to a regular pair of shoes. He calls it the Lunocet.

chapter one

Swimmers reportedly can reach up to 8 miles (12 kilometers) per hour using the Lunocet, which is made of carbon fiber and fiberglass.

In 2017, retired Olympic champion Michael Phelps tried the Lunocet. Many people consider Phelps the greatest swimmer in history. With the fluke on his feet, Phelps zoomed at nearly twice his normal speed. He easily beat his best Olympic times.

When someone finds a better way to do something, it's called **innovation**. Ted Ciamillo is an innovator. His Lunocet offers us a way to swim faster and farther.

Innovation is the driver of progress. Think about cross-country travel. Two hundred years ago, people traveled to California by horse and wagon. Their hard journey lasted six months. Later, railroads came along and cut the trip to about a week.

Today, jets enable us to eat breakfast in New York and have dinner in Los Angeles.

Swimming Machine

Ideas from Nature

Some of the best innovations come from plants and animals. Borrowing ideas from nature is called **biomimicry**. (*Bio* means "life" and *mimic* means "to copy.") The Lunocet, which copies a dolphin's fluke, is an example of biomimicry.

Our species, *Homo sapiens*, first appeared about 200,000 years ago. Other creatures have been here much longer. Beetles, for instance, began crawling around roughly 300 million years ago. Since then, beetles have developed many clever survival methods.

A dolphin's flukes are basically wings. Ted Ciamillo realized that the tails of dolphins work the same way in the water as airplane wings do in the sky.

chapter one

African desert beetles have one of the best tricks. They capture water from the air. During early morning fogs, the beetle raises its back into the air. Tiny water droplets slowly gather on ridges on the beetle's back. When the droplets get large enough, they roll down to the beetle's mouth so it can have a drink.

In 2016, researchers at Harvard University created a material for collecting water from air. Their design copied the desert beetle's shell. It can help people living in **arid** parts of the world.

The dime-size *Stenocara* beetle lives in one of the hottest and driest places on our planet, the Namib desert in southwest Africa. This desert only gets a half an inch of rainfall per year.

Swimming Machine

Dolphins and whales evolved from a wolf-like land animal. This ancestor, Pakicetus, had a taste for fish. As it spent more time in the water, **its body adapted to swimming.** Front legs became flippers. Fur gave way to thick skin with a layer of fat (called blubber) for warmth. **Dolphins and whales must surface for air or they will drown.**

Dolphins evolved into their current form about 5 million years ago. During that time, they too have developed some amazing survival skills.

2nd CHAPTER

Ocean of Ideas

Barnacles are shelled creatures that cling to flat surfaces. They like to hitch a ride on boat **hulls**. Too many barnacles can slow a ship.

In 2001, a group of German scientists studied the problem. They wondered how dolphins manage to stay barnacle-free.

The scientists placed a sample of dolphin skin under a microscope. They saw tiny ripples that deter barnacles. The scientists also found that dolphin skin oozes a slick gel. Barnacles cannot get a grip.

Their findings led to new paint for ship hulls. The slippery paint mimics dolphin skin to keep barnacles off boats. Traditional hull paint has harmful chemicals that leach into the sea. Dolphin-inspired paint is safe.

Saving the Sea

Humans rely on the ocean for food, oxygen, and medicine. Ingredients from the sea can be found in many products, from peanut butter to heart pills.

We know of roughly 230,000 **marine** species. Nobody can say how many more species might call the ocean home. Possibly millions, since scientists estimate that 95 percent of the ocean remains unexplored.

Pollution has become a major problem. Each year, billions of pounds of trash end up in the sea. Plastic junk causes the most concern because it breaks down into long-lasting flecks. Researchers have found traces of plastic in 114 different species, including many popular seafoods.

chapter two

Biomimicry can help us solve the plastic problem. In Portugal, a water bottle company used biomimicry to reduce its use of plastic.

Bottle designers looked to the white pine tree, which lives on windy mountaintops. The tree's spiral trunk can stand up to any gust. They copied the spiral shape to create a lighter, stronger water bottle. It saves 250 tons of plastic per year.

When doing their research, the bottle designers went to AskNature.org. It is an online catalog of nature-inspired ideas. Science writer Janine Benyus cofounded the free site.

Back in 1997, Benyus wrote a book called *Biomimicry: Innovation Inspired by Nature*. Ever since, she has been urging people to borrow ideas from plants and animals, including the clever dolphin.

Ocean of Ideas

porpoise

dolphin

FUN FACT

Dolphins and **porpoises are close cousins**. Porpoises have shorter noses, smaller fins, and thicker bodies. They are just as smart as dolphins but tend to **behave more shyly**.

3rd CHAPTER

Sea Genius

On a sunny day in Brazil, some local fishermen wade into the ocean. Farther out, bottlenose dolphins are chasing a school of fish.

As the chase grows closer, the fishermen cast their nets. The fish panic, for now they are cornered. Most swim straight into the nets. Those fish that turn to flee end up in the waiting mouths of the dolphins.

Long ago, these fishermen and dolphins learned to work together. The partnership exists because dolphins are highly intelligent. They play with toys, solve puzzles, and recognize themselves in a mirror.

In Shark Bay, Australia, dolphins use tools to find food. They know that fish like to hide in the bay's many **crevices**. Jagged rocks and broken shells would cut the dolphin's nose, or beak. Before poking around, a dolphin will grab a sea sponge. The soft sponge protects its beak.

Dolphins live in tightly knit social groups called pods. They communicate with clicks and whistles, and even call each other by name. Many attempts have been made to decode dolphin speech. So far, none have succeeded.

The pod often hunts as a team. They swim in a tight circle, trapping a school of fish. Team members then take turns going inside the circle to feast. Dolphin intelligence and teamwork fascinate scientists.

chapter three

Bio Sonar

In 1960, biologist Kenneth Norris made a remarkable discovery. Norris believed that dolphins used more than just their eyes to hunt and navigate. He thought they might use **echolocation**, also called bio sonar.

To test his theory, Norris blindfolded a bottlenose dolphin. It swam normally and avoided objects. Norris then set up an underwater maze. The blindfolded dolphin found its way out with ease.

Today, we know a great deal more about bio sonar. Dolphins have an organ in their forehead called the melon. The clicks we hear dolphins make are sound waves specially tuned by the melon.

When a sound wave hits an object, it bounces back as an echo. The dolphin's brain uses these echoes to paint a picture of the world around it.

Dolphin sonar is extremely accurate. Dolphins can detect a golf ball at 100 yards (91 meters). Plus, they can tell the difference between a golf ball and a Ping-Pong ball. One is dense and the other is hollow, so the balls have two different echoes.

FUN FACT

Dolphins have some of the biggest brains—relative to body size—in the animal kingdom. The brain of a bottlenose dolphin is **larger than a human brain!**

4th CHAPTER

Superb Seekers

Gentle waves lap against a small boat in San Diego Bay. It is July 2018. Nearby, dozens of huge warships perform a training mission.

The two people aboard the little boat have a mission too. They are dolphin trainers working for the U.S. Navy. Today, they are teaching a bottlenose dolphin to spot undersea mines.

Hidden mines pose a grave risk to ships. The Navy's best sonar devices have trouble locating them. For dolphins, it is easy.

The dolphin surfaces and signals it has found a mine. The trainers give it a marker, which it places near the dummy mine for divers to find later. The trainers **lavish** their student with praise and fish treats.

Some animal rights groups criticize the Navy's use of dolphins. Trainers reply that the dolphins get excellent care and seem to enjoy the challenge. In recent years, the Navy has tried switching to mine-hunting drones. To date, no drone can match the superb skills of a dolphin.

A trained dolphin reacts to hand gestures.

chapter four

Tsunami Warning

A tsunami is an unusually large sea wave. It comes from undersea earthquakes and volcanoes.

Tsunamis can be deadly to people on the coast. In 2004, an Indian Ocean tsunami killed almost 230,000 people in 11 different countries. With more warning, many of those victims might have escaped.

A German company called EvoLogics has created an early warning system for tsunamis. The EvoLogics designers spent eight years studying dolphins. Their system uses underwater sensors.

Superb Seekers

In 2014, an EvoLogics sensor detected a tsunami near Japan. It started after an earthquake rocked the sea floor off the coast of Chile. The tsunami, which missed Japan, proved the warning system works. However, the world's oceans are vast. **Deploying** enough sensors will take time.

Fortunately, the orca might be able to help. Orcas are dolphins, not whales, and they have terrific hearing. Researchers at Stanford University created an undersea microphone based on orca ears. The pea-sized microphone works in the deepest water and detects the softest whisper. Someday, it might warn us of distant tsunamis.

chapter four

Superb Seekers

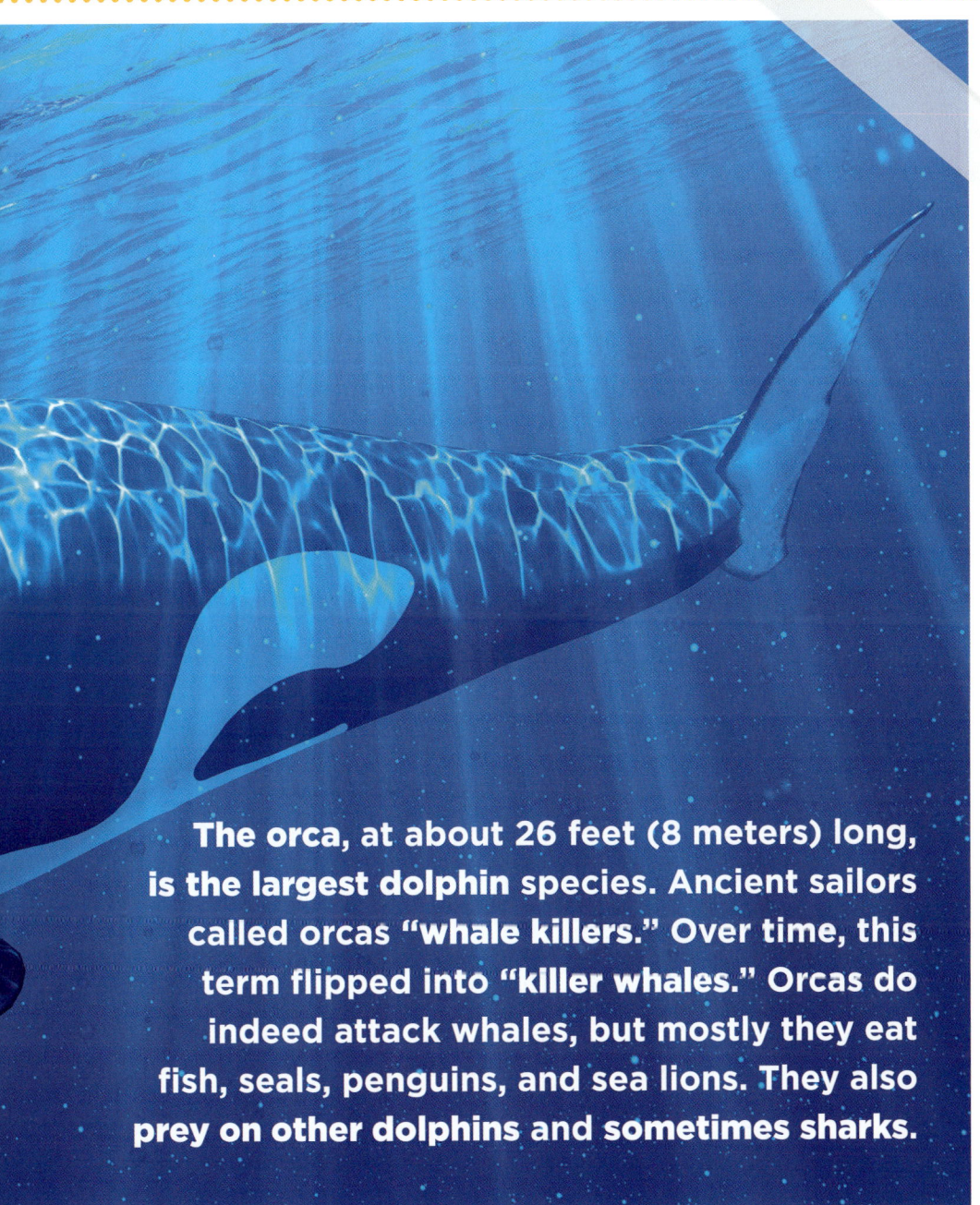

The orca, at about 26 feet (8 meters) long, is the largest dolphin species. Ancient sailors called orcas "whale killers." Over time, this term flipped into "killer whales." Orcas do indeed attack whales, but mostly they eat fish, seals, penguins, and sea lions. They also prey on other dolphins and sometimes sharks.

5th CHAPTER

Deep Discoveries

At a marine lab in Long Beach, California, researchers put a mirror in the water. Curious dolphins immediately approach. They take turns looking in the mirror, fascinated.

The researchers see unusual behavior from the dolphins. One hovers before the mirror, wiggling its flippers. Another opens its mouth to have a look inside. A third dolphin pivots to get a view of its belly. These acts suggest the dolphins know they are looking at themselves.

Few species can recognize themselves in a mirror. Scientists study the **cognitive** ability of dolphins to learn more about complex brains, including our own.

Brain Buddies

The brain is a mysterious organ. The more we learn about it, the more questions we have. Consider memory. Have you ever forgotten someone's name? Dolphins do not appear to have that problem.

Every dolphin has a unique whistle that serves as its name. When a dolphin's friends want it, they mimic its whistle and it answers. In 2013, scientists tested the bottlenose dolphin's ability to remember the whistles of friends it hasn't seen in years.

Just like humans, dolphins pick and choose their friends. And they can remember their friends after 20 years apart!

chapter five

The experiment focused on aquarium dolphins. Aquariums trade dolphins all the time for breeding purposes. As a result, friends may become separated. Scientists placed a speaker in the water and played whistles recorded at other aquariums.

The dolphins ignored the unfamiliar whistles of strangers. However, when they heard the whistle of an old friend, they grew very excited. They called back to the speaker. Some even slapped their tales in anger when the speaker was removed.

In one instance, the dolphins reacted to a whistle they had not heard in more than 20 years. No other species (beyond humans) is known to have such a good social memory.

Dolphins have inspired an artificial fluke for swimmers. They have shown us how to keep barnacles off boat hulls. Dolphin sonar holds clues for better navigation and tsunami detection. But their greatest gift may be yet to come. Dolphins might help us unravel mysteries of the mind.

Biomimicry is the act of copying nature to solve human problems. Natural solutions do not harm the environment. With biomimicry, people in science and business are finding tomorrow's ideas today.

What You Should Know

Dolphins are among the most intelligent species in the animal world. By studying them, we may gain insight into human memory and thought processes.

Innovators have mimicked dolphin tails, skin, and **sonar** to create useful new products.

Huge amounts of trash end up in the ocean every year. Scientists have found traces of plastic in 114 marine species.

Dolphins live in social groups called pods. They cooperate with each other (and sometimes with humans) to catch more fish.

The smart ideas that come from biomimicry have an extra benefit. They are safe for the environment.

Want to be an engineer? Architect? Inventor?

1. **Take math** and **science** classes
2. **Enroll in art** and **design** classes
3. **Attend STEM** camps and programs
4. **Visit nature preserves** and **parks** to observe nature at work
5. **Keep a journal** or a **blog** of your observations
6. **Enter science fairs** and **competitions**
7. **Check out books** on **biomimicry** from your school and public library
8. **Visit natural history museums** and **science centers**
9. **Check your community's calendar** for talks by **science** and **technology experts**
10. **Volunteer for citizen science events** like **bird counts**, **water sample collection**, and **weather reporting**

Glossary

arid
Extremely dry

biomimicry
Borrowing ideas from nature

cognitive
Relating to perception, memory, judgment, and reasoning

crevice
A crack, cleft, or fissure

deploy
To spread out or arrange

echolocation
Method of locating an object based on the echo it returns

hull
The main body of a ship, including the bottom, sides, and deck

innovation
To create or improve an object or method

lavish
Given in large amounts

marine
Existing in or produced by the sea

Online Resources

Visit the Conservationist for Kids webpage
www.dec.ny.gov/education/40248.html for more information about: Biomimicry, Green Chemistry, Green Schools, and Sustainability

Check out the Ask Nature website
www.asknature.org

Listen to Janine Benyus talk about biomimicry
www.ted.com/speakers/janine_benyus

Enjoy the podcast *30 Animals That Made Us Smarter*
www.bbc.co.uk/programmes/w13xttw7

Visit www.uspto.gov/kids/Biomimicry.pdf

Learn amazing facts about the bottlenose dolphin
kids.nationalgeographic.com/animals/mammals/bottlenose-dolphin/

Further Reading

Becker, Helaine, and Alex Ries. *Zoobots: Wild Robots Inspired by Real Animals*. Kids Can Press, 2014.

Koontz, Robin. *Nature-Inspired Contraptions*. Rourke Educational Media, 2018.

Perez Valice, Kim, and Andy Comins. *The Orca Scientists*. HMH Books for Young Readers, 2018.

Swanson, Jennifer, and Justine Jackson-Ricketts. *Absolute Expert: Dolphins*. National Geographic Children's Books, 2018.

Index

barnacles	10, 26
Benyus, Janine	12
Ciamillo, Ted	4, 6, 7
Lunocet	4, 6, 7
Norris, Kenneth	16
orca	21-23
Phelps, Michael	6
sonar	16, 18, 26, 28
tsunami	20, 21, 26

About the Author

Jim Corrigan has been writing nonfiction for more than 20 years. He holds degrees from Penn State and Johns Hopkins. Jim became a fan of biomimicry while working on a book about airplanes. He currently lives near Philadelphia.